About this book

Venomous snakes are sophisticated killers, attacking swiftly and sinking venom into their prey. Venom can kill, paralyse or momentarily blind a victim. Cobra and mamba snakes have fangs like a hypodermic syringe for injection of their lethal venom, which may cause heart or respiratory failure. The rattlesnake sounds a sinister warning when it is alarmed, by vibrating the rattle at the end of its body. In this book you can find out about venomous snakes from many parts of the world, which may often be beautifully marked – but deadly.

About the author

Dr Bernard Stonehouse is the author of many publications on ethology and ecology, and is Editor of the series *Biology and Environment*. He is Chairman of the Postgraduate School of Studies at the University of Bradford. His main interest is in environmental and natural history education. He is the author of several other books in this series.

Venomous Snakes

Bernard Stonehouse

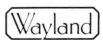

Animals of the World

ISBN 0 85340 846 7
© Copyright 1981 Wayland Publishers Limited

First published in 1981 by
Wayland Publishers Limited
49 Lansdowne Place, Hove
East Sussex BN3 1HF, England

Phototypeset by Trident Graphics Limited
Reigate, Surrey, England
Printed in Italy by G. Canale & C.S.p.A., Turin
Bound in the U.K. by The Pitman Press, Bath

Contents

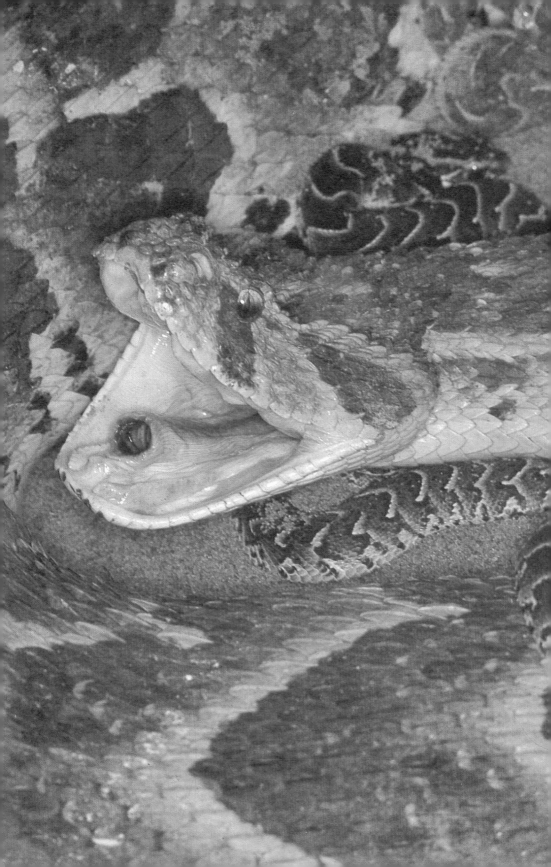

1 Danger – venomous snakes

Tropical adventure stories are never complete without some mention of venomous snakes – evil, slithering reptiles that hang from the trees or hide in somebody's bed, just waiting for a chance to strike. The snakes are always described as brightly coloured and fast-moving, and you know that anyone who gets bitten will die in agony, while the snake slides off hissing, in search of its next victim.

So many people have been bitten by snakes, that we know we must treat them with great care, but it is a mistake to think of every snake as poisonous or dangerous. Many very beautiful and completely harmless snakes are killed every year by people who believe them to be deadly. This is a pity, because snakes are interesting animals, with very highly-specialized bodies, and they are fascinating to watch as they go

A puff adder, a snake of the African plains, seen with its newly-born young.

9

The timber rattlesnake's fangs swing forward when it opens its mouth, ready to bite deeply

about their business. Far from being evil or aggressive, snakes are very timid animals that keep out of your way if they possibly can, and never strike at Man unless they are frightened and confused.

One of the best places to see snakes is in the tropics. Imagine a bright, cloudless morning on the African savannah, the air still cool after a clear night, the ground still damp with heavy dew. The birds are awake early and flying about, ready for the first feed of the day. They are warm-blooded, and so have a high body temperature despite the cold. Insects and lizards

10

are still sluggish in the chilly air, and can easily be picked off by the birds as soon as it is light enough to see them.

Snakes are cold-blooded animals, and unlike warm-blooded birds and mammals, they cannot keep up a high body temperature overnight. They are just as sluggish as the insects at day-break. But as soon as the sun appears and the air and ground start to warm, they emerge from holes in the ground, and cracks and crevices among the rocks where they have been sleeping overnight, and begin to bask in the early morning sun. As they warm up they become more lively, breathing faster and moving to warmer spots, looking about with watchful eyes in case

A green tree snake of Africa, showing that it can swallow a frog much wider than itself

an enemy has spotted them.

A thin green snake, no thicker than a broom handle and almost as long, suddenly appears at the foot of a tree. Clinging to the smooth bark like the stem of a climbing plant, it climbs easily, gliding upward with little effort until it is lost among the branches and leaves. Then it reappears, sliding out along a branch, rearing up and slipping on to the next branch above.

The black coachwhip snake gets its name from its thin whip-like body. This one is drinking

12

A forest cobra of India, rearing up and ready to strike

13

Eventually it comes to rest with the rear half of its body anchored firmly among the leaves and twigs, and the front end of its body hanging in mid-air. A passer-by would not see it at all, so perfectly does it match its background. Someone climbing in the trees might think it was a broken branch; a bird might even perch on it.

This is a boomslang, one of Africa's many species of poisonous tree snake. Its scaly green head conceals fangs – long, curved needle-sharp teeth with glands containing venom or poison near their roots. The snake watches with steady, unblinking yellow eyes as birds, lizards and small squirrel-like rodents come and go among the branches. Suddenly its head jerks forward and it grabs a chameleon, in a movement too quick for the eye to see. This grey-brown, pop-eyed lizard was itself slowly stalking insects among the branches.

The rest is a drama in slow motion. The chameleon struggles, but the boomslang holds it in vice-like jaws, suspending it helplessly in mid-air so that its claws cannot grip the branches. The chameleon kicks and lashes its tail, but the snake holds on. Gradually the

This African boomslang has caught a chameleon and is swallowing it head-first

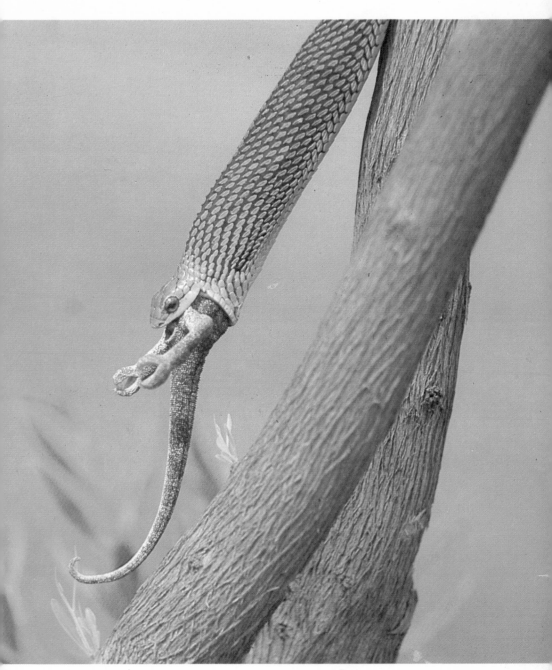

15

Slender tree or vine snakes of Central America. These back-biting snakes feed mainly on lizards

chameleon droops. The venom injected by the snake's fangs flows slowly through its veins; its twitching ceases, its eyes roll for the last time, and it dies. The poison seldom takes more than two or three minutes to work.

Now the snake rests on the branch and works the chameleon round in its mouth until it holds the head. Though the prey is more than twice as wide as the boomslang, and much bigger than its mouth, the snake gradually works its jaws forward over it, first the lower jaw, then the upper, the two sides of the jaws seeming to slide

16

forward alternately. As if by magic the chameleon slowly disappears; in less than an hour it is just a large bulge inside the snake, with only the tip of its tail still showing. The boomslang turns and glides away, in search of a quiet corner where it can digest its breakfast in peace. It will not need another meal for several more days.

A newly moulted boomslang of Africa, with its complete moulted skin beside it

2 How snakes evolved

There are about 3,000 different kinds or species of snake that live all over the world, in temperate and tropical lands. Snakes belong to the group of animals called reptiles. Their closest kin are the lizards, and more distantly, they are related to turtles, tortoises and crocodiles. Reptiles are vertebrates – backboned animals – with a vertebral column made up of bony blocks. They have a strong skull that protects the brain, a scaly skin, and usually two pairs of limbs. Over many millions of years of evolution snakes have developed a long, thin body and a flimsy skull, and have lost their limbs altogether. It is the lack of limbs especially, that makes them look quite different from other reptiles, though they still have the reptilian scaly skin.

Reptiles are a very ancient group. We know from fossils that the first ones appeared on earth

Snakes sometimes emerge together from warm places where they have been spending the night

over 250 million years ago, and they became a much larger and more varied group than they are today. Two hundred million years ago the group included the great dinosaurs – huge reptiles much bigger than elephants – as well as many smaller types. The first lizards appeared about 150 million years ago. In contrast to the giants they were light and agile little animals that could run up and down trees and scamper over the ground after insects, just as their descendants do today. The first snakes appeared about 120 million years ago, though they remained very rare for a long time. They

became plentiful 60 to 70 million years ago. By this time the big reptiles had disappeared altogether, and there were many more small, insect-eating mammals and birds. Snakes probably evolved as hunters of these small animals.

How did snakes evolve from lizards? We think the ancestors of snakes were particular kinds of lizard that took to living underground in burrows. Many snakes and lizards live this way today. A long, thin body is a very great asset for burrowing, but limbs tend to get in the

This black cobra keeps its head high as it swims across a flooded field

way; so over many hundreds of generations, the burrowing lizards became longer while their limbs became smaller. Modern lizards that live underground in burrows tend to be worm-like, with tiny limbs or no limbs at all.

Instead of walking, the early snakes would slither over the ground on their bellies, and the most flexible ones would be the most successful at catching their prey and sliding away from predators. Slowly these snakes developed the other specializations that make their descendants so efficient – special sensory organs, camouflage, hunting behaviour, flexible jaws, and in some families very effective venom and fangs for injecting it. Poison fangs are probably quite a recent development in the life history of snakes – a new weapon in their armoury for catching prey and defending themselves against attack.

Snakes have several ways of moving. Some of the biggest ones hold their body almost straight and glide forward by tiny rippling movements of their skin. Smaller ones throw their body into curves, shifting forward by pressing back against the soil or grass through which they are moving. The sidewinders raise their body partly off the ground, a useful trick for travelling over

*Sidewinder snakes move sideways across the desert,
keeping as much of their body as they can off the hot sand*

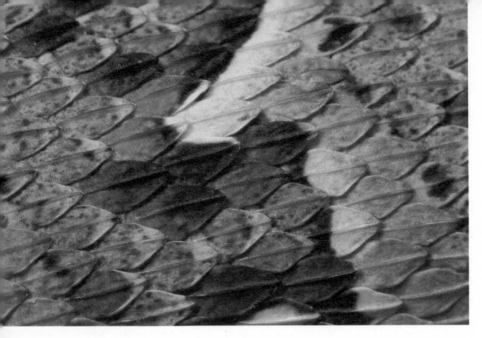

The beautifully-marked scales of a puff adder

hot desert sand. Snakes can move very rapidly if necessary; they twist and turn and disappear quickly into crevices or long grass, and are among the hardest animals of all to catch. It is surprising to see how well they climb, on rocks or in the branches of trees, and most snakes swim well – they often have to swim during the rainy season.

Their shiny waterproof skin is made up of tiny scales, often brightly coloured, that overlap or lie edge-to-edge in a thin outer layer of softer skin. Every year, or sometimes more often, snakes shed their outer layer of skin. A freshly-moulted snake always looks bright and shiny, gradually growing faded and shabby as

24

its skin ages. Snakeskin – the scaly layer – can be tough enough to tan, to make fine-quality leather. Many kinds of snake are hunted for their beautiful skins, which are made into shoes, handbags and other fashion goods.

Internally, snakes have a slightly different bone structure from other reptiles. They have more vertebrae than lizards; some of the biggest ones have over 400, each one with a pair of ribs. The vertebrae link together with complex joints, making them strong but flexible. Snakes

A pilot black snake, shedding its skin. The new skin underneath is bright and shiny

Above *This young rhinoceros viper has choked to death in trying to swallow a rat too big for it*

Below *Puff adders may give birth to 60 or 70 young at a time*

have no shoulder bones, and only a few have remnants of pelvic bones. The skull is made up of thin, flexible bones held together by elastic ligaments, enabling it to stretch in all directions when the snake is eating prey bigger than itself.

The snake's internal organs have become smaller and rearranged to fit into the long, slender body shape. Many snakes have only one lung, the gut is straight instead of being coiled, and the paired kidneys and reproductive organs are lined up behind each other instead of side by side. Most snakes lay eggs. Some keep the eggs inside them until they are ready for hatching, then give birth to live young.

An Indian small-spotted coral snake defending her two soft-shelled eggs

3 Why are snakes venomous?

All snakes are active hunters, that kill their prey and swallow it whole. But how do they catch prey, and hold it long enough to kill and eat it, if they slither over the ground and have neither hands nor arms? Snakes have several special organs and patterns of behaviour that help them to hunt efficiently.

They have no eyelids; a snake's eyes are protected by a transparent layer of skin that gives them their fixed, glassy stare. They probably see things rather indistinctly (some species are almost blind), but their eyes are sharp enough to detect slight movements. If you stand perfectly still when you see a snake, it may well not be able to see you at all, but it will pick up a movement of your hand straightaway, and possibly come and see if you are something to eat.

Snakes have no ear apertures or eardrums on

The extended fangs of a rhinoceros viper. The 'horn' on the tip of the nose is made up of hard scales

the sides of their head. Together with the lack of eyelids, this is a sure way of telling the difference between a snake and some of the legless lizards and blindworms that look rather like snakes. We hear sound waves in the air, but snakes feel sound through the ground, picking up dull vibrations mainly through their lower jaw.

Their tongue is very sensitive; the forked tip darts in and out of their mouth as they move, sampling the air and carrying molecules of 'taste' back to a sensory patch in the roof of the mouth. This may tell them when they are close to prey. Some of the most advanced snakes, the

A black mamba – one of the biggest of Africa's venomous snakes, that grows to 3 metres or more

A timber rattlesnake with tongue extended; the pit below the eye is sensitive to heat

pit vipers and pythons for example, can detect heat. Special heat-sensitive organs in tiny hollows or pits in their cheeks, tell them when they are close to a warm-blooded mammal or bird, or an egg, even in the darkness of an underground burrow.

Snakes can move fast, but not usually fast enough to chase down their prey. Instead they wait until the prey approaches them. Some snakes, like the boomslang, lie quietly and rely on their brown or green colouring to camouflage them. Some move their head or tail rhythmically, arousing the curiosity of birds and small

31

mammals and attracting them closer. Then the snake strikes hard with its head and neck. Mice, small birds, lizards and insects can be knocked off balance or stunned in this way, and small ones are swallowed immediately.

Non-venomous snakes often kill larger animals by throwing their body around them in coils and squeezing hard, preventing their breathing. This is how boas, pythons and other 'constrictors' cope with hares, small antelopes,

A coral snake, a small burrowing snake of the southern United States, with strong warning coloration

This flying snake has tackled and killed a gecko (lizard) much bigger than itself

even crocodiles, once they have caught them. Venomous snakes like the African boomslangs inject poison.

The poison glands which make the venom are specially modified salivary glands, and the venoms vary in their power and how they affect the prey. Some paralyse the muscles, some affect nerves or blood vessels. The venom prevents the prey from escaping, either by putting it to sleep, paralysing it or making it breathless. The animal cannot struggle, or run far even if it breaks away from the snake's jaws.

33

In some venomous snakes, which biologists think of as 'primitive' or closest to the ancestral kinds, the venom runs down grooves in the back teeth. Boomslangs are one of these 'back-biters', and generally strike only at animals small enough to fit into their mouth. More advanced snakes – rattlesnakes and vipers, for example – inject venom with their front teeth, which are long and curved, and swing forward into position when the snake opens its mouth. These 'front-biters' can tackle much bigger prey, and are often the most dangerous to Man and other large animals. They bite and then retreat, waiting for the venom to take effect before returning to finish their meal.

Boomslangs and other small snakes rarely strike at anything they cannot eat, except in self-defence; attacking larger animals would be a waste of valuable venom. Many of them hiss or rattle their tails noisily in warning when they feel threatened. Some snakes with dangerous venom are brightly coloured, warning all other animals to leave them strictly alone. However, these snakes have been known to bite cattle, antelopes and monkeys, and even people who have been unlucky enough to tread on them or grasp them accidentally while climbing trees.

A puff adder's head; there are no eyelids, and the broad cheeks contain the poison glands

This cobra has been killed by a mongoose — the main enemy of snakes

Their venom can be strong enough to kill a man or large animal.

Non-venomous snakes too may bite in self-defence, inflicting ragged wounds that soon heal if they are kept clean. So people all over the world tend to be wary of any snake, even the tiny ones that are only big enough to grasp a finger, wrist or ankle. Non-venomous snakes are often mistaken for venomous species.

36

Man is probably the snakes' most serious enemy, though many other species are snake predators. Birds of prey – owls, hawks, eagles, harriers and falcons – swoop down and attack snakes; if they can grasp them behind the neck, in their talons or beak, they cannot be bitten, and a captured snake is easily broken or chopped into pieces. Some mammals – especially mongooses – are great hunters of snakes. But so are other snakes; almost any species of snake will attack and kill another snake, and many that specialize in snake-killing (for example the king snakes of North America) are practically immune to the venom of the species which they live on.

4 Colubrids and cobras

The three thousand or more species of living snake are grouped by biologists into ten families. Of these, six are entirely non-venomous and three entirely venomous. The largest family of all – the Colubridae, with about 2,500 species – includes many non-venomous forms and a few hundred venomous, all of them back-biters.

Colubrid snakes are found in temperate and tropical regions all over the world, from the tip of South America to Canada, from South Africa, India and Australia to central Norway, Russia and Japan. The venomous colubrids tend to live in the warmest regions; examples of these are boomslangs of Africa and vine snakes; sand snakes and tree snakes are others. These usually have two or three grooved teeth on either side of the upper jaw, and relatively weak

The hood of an Indian cobra is supported by spreading ribs, making the snake look bigger and more dangerous

*The Montpellier snake is a small venomous snake of
southern Europe*

40

A paradise tree snake – one of the flying snakes of
south-eastern Asia

venom. Often they have to chew their victims,
injecting several lots of venom into them, before
they succumb.

One of the larger venomous colubrids is the
Montpellier snake, found in many warm countries of the Mediterranean area. A brown or
green snake, reaching lengths of up to 2 metres
(6 feet), it lives on birds, rats, lizards and other
snakes, first immobilizing them with its venom
and then returning to swallow them. The tree
snakes of India, Sri Lanka and Indonesia live
like the boomslangs, catching all kinds of small
prey far above the forest floor. Among them are

the curious flying snakes, that climb high in the trees and jump from branch to branch like coiled springs. Occasionally they glide, leaping from a high branch and flattening themselves in mid-air to form a sail; if they catch the wind, they may even soar slightly before landing in another tree several hundred metres away. Flying allows them to travel long distances and explore several trees without coming down to the ground.

The cottonmouth is a dangerous snake found in the swamplands of the southern United States

A long-nosed tree snake. Females of this species are longer than males, and may reach almost two metres

Another interesting group of colubrids from the same part of the world are the fishing snakes. There are several species, and they live most of their lives in the shallow waters of streams, lakes and canals. Some fishing snakes have tentacles on their noses; they are said to wiggle these in the water to lure small fish to within striking distance. Fishing snakes feed mainly on fish, frogs and other freshwater prey that they catch among the reeds and stones.

The snakes of the Elapidae family are found in more tropical areas. The best known among

44

them are the Indian cobras – the ones often seen performing with snake charmers – but the cobras as a family are found in the warmer parts of both North and South America, Africa and southern Asia. Cobras have large, fixed, poison fangs in the front of their jaw. Each fang is a tube with a central canal, that leads the venom down from the poison gland and injects it into the wound.

Indian cobras grow to lengths of 2 metres (6 feet). When disturbed or threatened they can raise the front half of their body vertically and spread their 'hood' – a broad flange on either side of the neck, supported internally by ribs. Often the hood has a pattern on the back like a pair of eyes, making it look more fearsome. Cobras are not especially fierce snakes, but there are many millions of them in India living among a very large human population. Every year ten thousand or more people are estimated to die from cobra bites, mostly inflicted when they are walking about barefooted in the dark. Cobras lay eggs in nests of leaf-mould, and the mother cobra guards them until they hatch.

Kraits and king cobras of Asia, taipans and

A spitting cobra can shoot a fine spray of venom from its fangs – a good way to keep enemies at a distance many lesser species of Australia, coral snakes of North America and mambas of Africa are all part of the Elapidae family. These are all venomous, and their bites can prove fatal to Man. King cobras are among the largest venomous snakes reaching up to 4 metres (13 feet) in length; mambas may grow even bigger, though large ones are rare nowadays after generations of heavy hunting. Several kinds of African cobra

The banded krait is a highly venomous species with a 'keel' or sharply-ridged back

*An African green mamba searching for eggs and small
birds among nests of woven grass*

have developed the trick of spitting venom.
Opening their mouths wide, they apply muscu-
lar pressure to their poison glands and shoot out
a jet that can travel several metres. The venom
is an irritant to the skin, and very painful if it
hits the eyes or nostrils. These snakes probably
use it to keep dangerous predators – birds,
mammals, or even other snakes – at bay.

5 Sea snakes, vipers and rattlesnakes

Sea snakes form a separate family of snakes (Hydrophidae) found only in the warmer parts of the Indian and Pacific Oceans, from the coast of Africa to South America. One species, the black and yellow sea snake, is found in both oceans, from Madagascar in the west to Panama in the east. Other species are more restricted in range. Though often found near the coast, they can live far out at sea; there are occasional reports of tens of thousands of brightly-coloured sea snakes basking on the surface of a warm ocean in the early morning sunlight.

Sea snakes live on fish, which they seem to catch mostly in shallow water. They are often found lurking in coral reefs, weaving in and out of the coral, snapping at the browsing fish. Fishermen often bring them up in their nets. Sea snakes are venomous, usually equipped

The cottonmouth gets its name from the white mouth that shows when the snake threatens or strikes

with strong poisons that knock out their prey in a matter of seconds. They are occasionally reported to bite swimmers, especially skin-divers who interfere with them. They swim freely; most species have a flattened tail, which wags from side to side in the water and drives them forward at a good pace. Some species come ashore to lay eggs, which they bury in the warm sand. Others are viviparous, producing their young alive in the water. They come up to

A banded sea snake exploring the sea bed for food. These snakes are often found on coral reefs

A puff adder on a desert soil; its patterned skin is good camouflage in bright sunlight

the surface to breathe air, but can stay below for many hours, especially when they are inactive. The biggest can measure 3 metres (9 feet) long.

Vipers – snakes of the family Viperidae – are in many ways the most advanced of all the snakes. They live in Europe, Africa, America and Asia; nearly all are terrestrial, short and rather thick-bodied, with very long fangs that shoot forward when the mouth opens, and fold away like knife-blades when it shuts. A typical small example is the European viper, familiar on dry, warm heathlands in Britain and

A pit viper – the heat-sensitive pit can clearly be seen between eye and nostril

throughout Europe, even as far north as central Norway. The name 'viper' indicates the way these snakes breed; they are viviparous, producing a few living young each season.

European vipers (also called adders) can often be seen sunning themselves on warm spring days, They feed on lizards, mice and frogs, possibly taking ground-nesting birds and their eggs as well. In autumn they give birth to between fifteen and twenty young, and in late autumn they hibernate, usually in burrows deep underground. Their bite can be very painful, but is seldom fatal to Man. Many other species of viper, asp and adder live in the warmer countries further south, where they are generally active throughout the year. Puff adders of Africa, one of the largest and most dangerous species, reach lengths of almost 2 metres (6 feet): their venom is intensely poisonous and quick-acting, and accounts for many hundreds of human deaths every year.

The pit vipers form a subfamily of the Vip-

A horned adder swallowing a large desert mouse

eridae; they occur in Asia and America but not in Africa, and they all have the facial pits with which they detect the presence of warm-blooded prey. By far the best known of these very efficient snakes are the rattlesnakes of North America. They get their name from a 'rattle' of dried skin on the tail. Though many snakes shake their tail when alarmed, rattling leaves and pebbles, only rattlesnakes have a built-in warning device that gives a loud rattle even on dry sand.

Rattlesnakes and copperheads, two of North America's most dangerous snakes, live mainly in dry areas, particularly in the south. Copperheads hibernate in winter; rattlesnakes usually live in warmer, arid areas and tend to remain active through the year. There are several species of rattlesnake, the largest growing to about 1.5 metres (5 feet) long. They feed mainly on small rodents, lizards and rabbits. All have intensely poisonous venom, and if Man is the victim, a bite is painful and often deadly. Cottonmouths (so-called because of the white lining to the mouth) are swamp-living pit vipers of the southern United States. Fer-de-lance and bushmasters live further south in the fields and forests of South America.

54

*A diamond-backed rattlesnake; you can see the rattle on
the tip of the tail held in the air*

Man has lived close to poisonous snakes for long enough to know how to cope with their dangers. The best way is always to avoid them, walking carefully in snake country and wearing sensible boots and trousers to ward off possible attacks from the ground. If you are bitten, it is usually possible to minimise the danger by injecting anti-snakebite serum. People who travel regularly where there are snakes often carry this with them, and can inject it before the poison takes effect. Applying a tourniquet and making the wound bleed may also help to

Milking a cobra of its venom. Venom is used in preparing anti-snakebite serum

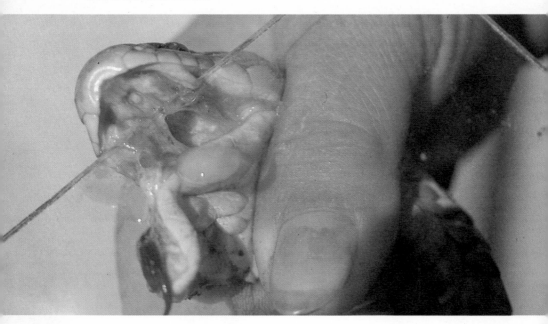

A copperhead snake; the frog has already been immobilized by venom, and will shortly be eaten

lessen the damage. Perhaps the most important point of all is – do not panic. Not every snake that bites is a venomous one; not every venomous snake is a killer. Knowledge is important; if you can identify the species that bit you, you may well find the doctor armed with a serum that will help you to a quick recovery.

Glossary

BACK-BITERS Snakes with *venom fangs* at the back of the mouth.

CAMOUFLAGE The colouring or pattern on an animal's body which helps it to escape notice by blending in with its background.

COLD-BLOODED A creature that takes its body temperature from the surrounding air.

EVOLUTION The process of change undergone by living creatures in the history of the world.

FANG A large pointed tooth. Venomous snakes have long hollow or grooved fangs, through which the venom is injected.

FOSSILS The remains, impression or trace of an animal or plant found preserved in rock.

FRONT-BITERS Snakes with *venom fangs* at the front of the mouth.

HIBERNATION The way some animals spend the winter in an inactive state resembling sleep.

LIGAMENT A band of strong elastic tissue connecting bones, cartilages, muscles etc.

POISON GLAND A gland, usually in a snake's head, that produces *venom*.

PREDATOR An animal that hunts and eats other animals.

PREY An animal that is hunted by a *predator* for food.

REPTILE A *vertebrate* animal with scaly skin. The family includes snakes, lizards, crocodiles, turtles.

SAVANNAH A wide expanse of green grassland with scattered bushes or trees.

SENSORY ORGAN A structure that allows an animal to receive sensations; like the eye, ear, nostril, skin.

SERUM A water fluid.

VENOM The poison produced by some animals and

VERTEBRATE An animal with a backbone, such as fish, frogs, reptiles, birds and mammals.

VIVIPAROUS A creature which gives birth to live young.

WARM-BLOODED An animal that keeps a high, constant body temperature.

Picture acknowledgements

All photographs from Bruce Coleman Limited, by the following photographers: Jen and Des Bartlett 8, 26 below; Rod Borland 23; Mark Boulton 15; John and Sue Brownlie 57; Jane Burton 20–21, 24, 35, 51; Peter Davey 30; Jack Dermid 42, 55; M. P. L. Fogden 12; C. B. Frith front cover, 27, 41, 43, 46, 52; David Hughes back cover, 53; Peter Jackson 38; Leonard Lee Rue III 10, 25, 31; J. Mackinnon 18, 33; Norman Myers endpapers, 11, 13, 17, 26 above, 28, 32, 36, 47, 56; G. D. Plage 44; Allan Power 50; Hans Reinhard 16, 40; John Shaw 48.

60

Index